ICE FISHING

Andrew Taylor

PAPERBACK POETS 15

UNIVERSITY OF QUEENSLAND PRESS

Published by University of Queensland
Press, St. Lucia, Queensland, 1973

Printed by Lantern Lithographics Pty. Ltd.
Bound by Gibbs and Podlich Pty. Ltd.

National Library of Australia card
number and ISBN 0 7022 0832 9

Designed by Cyrelle

Distributed in Britain, Europe, the
Middle East, Africa, and the Caribbean
by Angus & Robertson (U.K.) Ltd.,
2 Fisher Street, London, WCIR 4QA, England

Also by Andrew Taylor:
The Cool Change (Paperback Poets 4)

Acknowledgment is made to
the *Age*
Australian Poetry 1972 (Angus & Robertson)
Australian Poetry Now (Sun Books)
Chelsea (USA)
Choice (USA)
Meanjin Quarterly
New Poetry
Poet's Choice 1970, 1971 (Island Press)
Southern Review
Twentieth Century
We Took Their Orders and are Dead (Ure Smith)
the Australian Broadcasting Commission

Registered in Australia for transmisison by
post as a book

For Fred
who made it all come good

*Three moves in six months and I remain
the same.*
John Logan

*The greatest poverty is not to live
In a physical world, to feel that one's desire
Is too difficult to tell from despair.*
Wallace Stevens

Contents

Thirty

*Hope deferred maketh the heart sick: but when the desire cometh, it is
a tree of life.* Proverbs 13:12

One already seethes with green
but the rest are bare, black with grime and rain
or sketched with burgundy like a design
that tantalises sight so little's there
yet precedes the green.
Fitful rain
grass which is sodden slippery oblique
and overhead the bricks
of the rail bridge tattered into streaks.
I've walked out here in this slush weather because
it's spring and I'm thirty. Ahead
the prospect's not enchanted: increase
of pitched factories, rabble of elms
— one green the others black with rain —
a train bridge that never runs a train. No
shaft of light, no children
praising innocently in the waste.

Among elms
river useless bridge and mud I'm the one
disconsolate thing. I walk
sunk in my coat because to sit
home would be worse. I sat
most of today there, watching walls
stare back at me. Green paint
won't blossom, won't leaf. Out here
there's the raw air, crude sky,
an industrial forest of forgotten elms:
stripped twigs, whip saplings
tough wayward trees and the one
unaccommodated green
herald of spring at least!

whose sap rises like a dream toward home,
dreams of summers like honey in a shire,
some long-overtaken principality
milder, ancestral, intimate,
it will never see.
Its green is desire.

The beating

Beating her sensible with a storm of tissues
in the domestic paddock of their bed
while sheep rattled blathering over the pillows
out of sleep, and the light hung over them, a hawk,
a needle-point of sun, a rabbit's fear, a phrase,
— he whipped her into a souffle of delight,
took a new walk through an ancient city
and with Columbus tackled the Western Descent.
Stranded on Newfoundland, on the cold shore,
he stormed the Bastille, and sighed, and tucked the blankets in.
And when her boat drifted to Avalon,
her hair streaming goodbye across the sheet,
and samite mists descended and the Opera House
was a bootbox rattled by brooms, the chandeliers
aggressive bulbs choking in smoky heat,
he couldn't sleep, but walked the neighbouring room,
nursing the radio's small warm bleating defeat.

Corrections to a pastoral

1

A wren flits over water and sits still
on the stone parapet. Watchful her eye
half-way between clear water and a sky
shared by the afternoon shadow of a hill.
Half-moving, half-inert, on a frail claw
the wren's a thing of air that water and stone
have borrowed to commemorate the quiet
presence of sunlight by an open door.
Mid-afternoon. No-one moves about
in the restaurant. The wren gathers her crumbs.
A shout comes from the hillside, higher up.

2

A wren flits over water and sits still
on the stone parapet. Watchful her eye
half-way between sheer water and a sky
shorn by the bulked massif of a hill.
Half-moving, half-inert, rapid her claw,
the wren's a thing of air that water and stone
have borrowed to consolidate in one
sun's confidence beside an open door.
Mid-afternoon. No-one moves about
in the dark doorway. The wren busies with crumbs.
A shout comes from the hillside, high up, clear.
Nothing moves but the wren who, warily, comes
closer to stone's edge, water's, throwing out
with a head's toss, into sunlight, any fear.

3

. . . Nothing moves but the wren who, trembling, comes
closer to stone's edge, water's, sowing out
with a head's toss, into sunlight, fear . . . fear . . .

4

From the hill's face, close by, comes a shout . . .

Almost summer

Once more the old mechanism of earth
has persevered through a dozen wintry weeks
to its annual miracle. Tonight
insects clatter at the windows,
our kitten tires of chasing them and sleeps,
a panting orange comma of fatigue
temporarily fur.
Outside, everything's silk web.
The grapevine hosts small noises. Snails
venture their silvery tracks over the loam,
moths beat up from the dark, stars lean down
on the park opposite. The old house
breathes summer, the deep satisfying breath
of climbing roses indolent in heat,
leafed elms, grass mown, fresh and the scent
of lilacs searching the corridor's retreat
to where you lie, loose, tiredly asleep.
Earlier, sparrows chaffered in the leaves,
you shone with life that was blowing in the wind,
and where your glass had stood on the table
a small circle of moisture disappeared.
You pointed, laughed: 'It's almost summer' you said.

The old colonist

1

Our old tomcat, with his weak heart,
anything over eighty, though once
menace of the whole district, prefers
to piss in the sink, in the frypan,
on the vegetables.
Anything but go out in the rain
and cold. Anything
than go at all. We house him
now in the laundry, on an old cushion
on the antique copper. He pisses
on the soap, finally on the cushion.
The laundry was a hazard of stale shit. Yet
when we scrubbed it with disinfectant,
hosed out the stink, encouraged clean air in,
he was neither grateful nor malcontent,
but with ravelled, unwashed dignity,
intelligent eyes, and ears alert,
from great age and its obscurity
pissed on the ironing with deliberate intent.

2

six days later

Too old at last even to wash himself
his only thought was to be comfortable.
Mostly on the table under the vine
he lay on his side, watching all his years
slip quietly from him, kittens prowl
backyard and lane that had been once his pride.
His tail was a tattered skipping-rope,
his haunches rejects of an Op-Shop coat:
you almost thought the moths would pass him by
he was so tattered. Hardly weighed a pound.

He had stopped eating, would sniff milk, take
barely a bite to eat then turn away,
content that we had offered him the choice,
would purr when we coaxed him, but still turn away.
And yet he had his spirit to the end.
We used his table for our lunch, and found
him comfortable among the cutlery
minutes before the guests arrived — not once
but three times. Lunchtime yesterday. Our last
sight of him was a scornful rickety leap
over the fence, tail raised in a vague
vanishing salute. This afternoon
we found him, dead, ants beginning to swarm,
stretched in the sun, warrior to the last,
sprawled like an insult on the mayor's front path.

Invitation for midday

inner-urban address

1

Four above four, turning at the end
of the wide balcony, elegant sweep of sky,
eight stone arches, conjured from a mass
of climbing roses, feathery birch, ivy,
azaleas, daisies, clematis at the pier
of the doorstep — spring lingers here
through summer, as your house
marches Italianately into the past —
its colonnade, court, splash of a hidden fountain,
drone of bees. You stand
carefully on your top step welcoming guests —
the curious in the street cast half a glance
at the done-up house, its music and its ways —
lunch, and at midday Sunday,
thoroughly expected. So pleased
to see me come. From the street
into the dim 'salon' tinkling with drinks
I head unerringly for the makeshift bar.

2

Beyond the window a row of old
terraces take their autumnal light
like Chelsea pensioners regarding a display
by paratroops. Their eyes seem closed,
they doze as the bleak light batters down.
Ten blocks have been razed. I can smell
the sour stink of a smouldering house,
brick dust loiters on the sill as an old
car pulls to the kerb and a family
carrying a bunch of flowers

knocks at a door. The sun pours down
as you pour whisky, and someone says
something about the Housing Commission,
how 'even on Sunday they're still
knocking things down.' You pass drinks
shutting the window as you pass,
preferring the art of conversation
to demolition or conservation.

3

Your wife moves rapidly among her guests,
her nervous deprecating laughter shines
on polished surfaces, touches as the light
touches the fineness of her husband's taste.
She smokes too much, I notice, as she takes
my glass to be refilled; but then
I don't smoke anything, and so perhaps
smoking at all is too much. Maybe
you told her I was 'somebody'? — she stays
talking as though I were — too much
— and then: Why does she talk too much? The door
distracts, releases her. She roams,
a searching spirit through the bric-a-brac,
talking too much, too quickly, to be at home.

4

The table is of oak, you are proud
of the Persian rug on the wall, of the fine
old paintings, furnishings. Particularly
you enjoy my admiration
of the oak dresser in the kitchen
('an old aunt brought it from England')
of the glazed bookshelves, of a fine

escritoire. When lunch comes
it is served impeccably. I feel
I want far more to drink than I'll ever get
here, I'd like to get
very drunk and perhaps break
something of value
or an escritoire.

5

You start with a green bowl on the table.
You fill it
with persimmons, a dimpled
complexity of grapes,
peaches in a sunny shade, and beyond
like hills, the green immensities of
apples, pears . . .
Canyons
glitter as the rind catches
the day's heat.
Above
you pile a fantastic consciousness of air
where a citron eagle, poised upon a whim,
peers at the baffling crevices for prey.
He glides off as 'Now', you say, 'would you
care for some fruit?' The landscape
shifts a foot, your guest
chooses, and there's a bowl of fruit,
less an apple, before the window.

6

And in the drift of smoke
a pair of eyes, levelled over a glass,
seeks out their element. One moment

they meet mine, then
move on, perhaps looking for her husband?

7

After the goodbyes and thankyous
and promises of invitations
we find in the street that the 'march of time'
has taken a step closer. A red truck
filled with a house two blocks down shudders past
spilling a plaster corbel at my foot.
I kick it aside. A chipped nose and lip
catch what's left of the light. I take it up
instead and put it in the car. He stands
on his top step, waving goodbye, caught
in the same light. I wonder
what he would say if life caught him,
carried him away, what he would say
if I caught his wife up, leaving him
to hear the red trucks trundle rubbish past.
Would he sit there, serving lunch to friends
as demolition gangs hacked house by house
his century from under him? I wave
and drive too quickly with my battered mask,
weighing his lunch too heavy on my mind.

Clearing away

Today I chopped back irises
spear-sharp
layers of leaves
long as our memories —
Vietnam, savage green
in the March decline;
paler, lank low leaves
almost brittle — Korea;
then a tangle of grey —
dusty, forgotten rubbish —
the last war, Second World War —
crumbling to the blade.
Beneath —
the red-backed spider
angry at being disturbed.

Autumn thunder from Indo-China

Where afternoon smells of
burnt fallen leaves
raked to a suburban
offering to a year
and clover
foams underfoot
winter's unanswerable boom
echoes from the Sun King's
disintegrated empire

(bruised sky powerless to be mute)

its fragments
clatter like boots across the level
bed of our sheets
cats' shriek
addles love's harmonies

we play at soldiers
attack draw back thrust again
each autumn morning a hundred
corpses
furled in newspapers
wait on our lawn

Anthologised at last!

Introduction

Condemned by a terse
line and a half
into an ape's posture
        halfway down
        the tree of life
        conscientiously changing my mind

Text

in an octavo prison
my few little songs
various as a bellbird's

Postscript

        with their plastic spine
        paper from breast to back
will march into the Burwood library
the Indooroopilly library the Unley library
the Liverpool (NSW) library
        and will occupy a perch
        on a way-out twig of a remote
        branch of an unimportant
        branch library

Criticism

outside the trees will be waving
windily weaving birdsong into sky
my cat crawls up a trunk
hungry for birds
        their warm meat
        mouthy feathers
        giveaway chaffer

undigestible beaks and toes
my cat can't sing for his supper

History's verdict

I have
five poems in the public library
next to the supermarket
        the cashier with false eyelashes
        wouldn't credit a cheque from me
        even if I screwed her
        even if I sang about it

Prayer in autumn

Suetonius
O God of leather goods
and history
grant to my wife a new purse
and a lambskin coat
(fleece-lined)
against the winter
and for myself
grant me like Samuel Pepys
a hand-stitched
kidskin contraceptive
that I may take my fill of the world's
confusion
but not increase it.

Slide night

1

Examine my window carefully:
it is covered with grass — thrown up
by the mower and stuck because it was
even at 3.30 yesterday
still wet with dew. It's going brown.
Some insect has laid twelve rows
of eggs, fragment of a giant
thumbprint — nature's — in a corner.
It's dirty, and paint spatters it
from a bad paint job. Moths crawling.

2

Put it under the microscope.
Do you see the man, head full
of grass, moth eggs, paint,
sitting at a desk? See insects
clamber through his eyes, ferret his ears
for light, twaddle his page?
Stamped in one corner, Certified
Fit To Rage? A host of caterpillars
populate and perish out of that script?

3

Or flash it on a screen (memories
of the Uffizzi and/or was it Utrecht?)
a meadow scholar, flowery page be-sprent,
or a firm burgher, pastoralised.
In one corner the museum stamp,
inscrutable as a postmark from Taiwan.

4

From here, inside, it's largely black
— because it's night — and that's where you are,
all of you: in the dark! Moths,
heads ablaze, patrol my image
my giant ghost on the glass,
merino bodies quiver at my eye.
Larger than the huntsman I am the sky.
My galloping fingers sweep the universe. No stars.
Moths instead, heads flaming as Betelgeuse.

5

Switch out the show. It's time to sleep. To sleep.
My head expands to the brilliance of a quasar,
space swallows my wavelength, hour after hour.

In March

The buzzing furious atom of my heart
drove me about the circuit of despair
around the figure of love. From the start
in the small room of furniture, the cat
footing it after insects into air,
his fur hunger, ears a deadly device
to search out, kill, devour, his restless
movement trampled within my double heart.

Urged out by the night air in his eyes
I felt the night wind harrowing my hair
among lank olive outcrops — bitter fruit —
featureless rock, earth past form or care,
by a mad March torturing demiurge ripped and wrung —
angriest and most sad of winds,
it shredded summer from the sky all night
blew all the streetlamps' lighting out to space
hustled my footsteps farthest out, then back
to cracked earth, olive frenzy, the things
of stone kicked in the dark, the small
bedroom, the cat asleep.

Today I watched the spiral of a gull
over the grey level of waves
picking his prey with a cruel hurry of wings.
'Things move in circles' I said. You smiled
as though the remark had echoed from the far
edge of the universe and found you fair.

After Monday, New York

That scream high in the air
lights tunnelling through rock

under water under rock underneath silence
lights stop a noiseless
exasperation of newspapers baseball results
somewhere up in the air above
neon rock slime water there's
still daylight summer evening 7.30
Friday the subway jammed
rancid with heat frustration
anything to be out

Down here it is warm and still
totally black
all touch I am out of touch
my burrow I have found this out
three quarters round the world
the telegrams
shocked messages dead
I've gone to earth

Such a high
inaudible scream of death up there in air
cool tender twilight
not cool not tender but set against the edge
of my father's death it's polished brilliant and pale
Manhattan is as lucid as a shell
a nautilus poised one second on the shore

the wave of people below me surfaces
they are all alive
the thin wail of a plane drifts out to sea
Brooklyn a police syren
syrens
the hot road shudders and rumbles underneath
no more telegrams I pray please no more death

Ah, Brave New World

For my father: died 7 September 1970

1 The locked playground

There's a padlock, but the key is lost
the padlock rusted. Above,
trees tower, vaster than giants in the dark,
stride in a rush of twilight, crushing
and still miraculously preserve
our stolen, fragile tract where a glow
floats on the grass like mist — light
kindled by warm grass, tumbling, sweat,
excitement, magic. My first
trespass in heaven, and I left behind
the toll of innocence. Today, too,
the key's lost, the padlock
shapeless with rust, the trees immense,
while every year has reinforced the fence.

2 For Robin Hardiman

Five hours late and Kennedy underfoot
New York through piles of carpet and a wait
for baggage. Then outside
the dense night steamed with rain, a tropical
exotic argument over taxi-fares,
expressways skirting the whole universe.
West or north meant anything to me,
we navigated through a haze and kept
Manhattan to starboard, though we couldn't see
Manhattan. I could have been
Hannibal down from the Alps, approaching Rome
like Attila, moving toward those
dark unimaginable heights. Until
you gave a direction and we came aground

beside a sumac in an area.
We talked the rest of that night into a haze
of recognitions, memories — five
years'. You cut me down to bedsize,
giving New York just as you gave your home.

3

Fort Greene Park — the air heavy with ruin —
heroism martyrdom independence —
the monolith cracked, scribbled at the base,
inscriptions defaced, prised off, paving loose,
instead of leaves litter, the west wind wrappings.
Puerto Rican families picnicked, slept
in the hot shade, rank grass that sloped
to Myrtle and the gaunt ambitious stride
of the abandoned rusting never-arriving El.
Dog shit everywhere, and not all dogs'.
I saw a drunk sick forty-year-old whore
hefting her rancid thighs so that a drizzle
of piss ran through the slatted seat beside
the two blacks drinking from a bottle at her side.
And I'd come here to stifle a far death —
a telegram had laid me like a blade
of summer grass and I'd sought out the straight
uprightness of the living dead, the green
space, gesture to heaven, breath of living.

4

'Kiss him' my mother whispered, as I left.
Instead I did the manly thing,
grasped his hand, looked him in the eye
and left him stranded in the hotel foyer,
the noiseless attention of porters, the paid

plump leather chairs. So tearless,
just as he'd wanted me, I might have been
thirteen, leaving for boardingschool.
Instead New York; he, dead in seven days.
Two weeks before, I'd driven him shopping.
He'd walked the main street, raising his hat
to friends who hadn't seen him for three months.
I'd walked, tremored each step he took. Each step
was firm, firmer, further from the bed
I'd watched him nearly dead in. Someone
asked how he was recovering, and he'd smiled.

5

Openwindowed nights we'd float
high on the springy fragrance of grass
among soft stars, arches of elms
on toe-tip brushing their fingers at a breath
of forgotten fragmentary breeze.
Or down into rock — the subways' drilled
and shuddering fissures of a nerveway through
the inert body of night, to surface
at stabbing lights, battering of lights.
Slow mornings — hiss, rumble of a bus
hardly could jolt us upright. Nighttime
was our day, and the muttering rock
our body wakened out of ecstasy
as pain leapt like a fever borough to borough.
The elms' cool promises held even higher
than voyaging remedies like ours could flutter.

6

So far below, the sea was nothing but
scrapings of cloud, and the sky become
so lonely — an aspiration between
five hours of night and Hawaii's grit and surf
we were nowhere. Icarus could be begging a ride
down, any moment, through the numb windows.
The yawn of a new day. Our fellow
passengers stir into boredom, combing
their sleepy hair. Nowhere at all. Nowhere!
Somewhere along 7th Avenue I stare
at the blazon of a jet aimed higher and higher
above heaped sidewalks, blather of Times Square
the grey scramble of buildings into grey
watery sky, envying its
cloudlike arrogance of how we tread our late
mornings into later evenings and nights,
tossed on a sleepless grid above no fire.

7

East 88th, then through a tangle of elms
that left behind the entrances, the rows
of garbage cans, drip of the air conditioners,
scramble of traffic   an abrupt rise,
a wild uncertainty of leaves, suddenly
New York level as all honesty —
the central reservoir. Opposite,
towers of luminous stone refracted haze,
solid as mist they were another land
built out of promise and expectancy
across a space to breathe, a peace of water.
Pilgrim's vision of the Celestial City,
Avalon, wonderful because the sudden
lucidity of distance, water

kept them intact. Summer after summer
you'd drive us, restless with baggage, children all eyes,
round wrestling mountain roads — all at once
the sea fulfilled the valleys, impossibly high,
the car a boat adrift on a green tide.

8

Fog, a nicotinestained yellow fog
as we left Manhattan, the colour of
an old pipe-smoking gardener's
querulous talkative tremulous moustache.
New Jersey washed it to a swampy grey —
pipelines dodged along the throughway like
a highschool drop-out trying to sell a hot
watch, bad acid, a fake grandstand pass.
Past Paterson the fog was placid and white,
sumacs succumbed to elms, elms gave way
in their top boughs to a pearl sky, hills
were sudden mysteries, Rhinelands. Later
on the drifting flats the barns leapt past,
brown ruminants enshrouded in the vague
dreams of an estimate of winter and corn.
A whole day, a whole state in fog:
Buffalo was invisible; Canada,
crystalline as the Promised Land,
was two miles off into another world.

9 To Jill, in Buffalo

A trunk heavy with secrets blocks our hall,
its key lost between New York and here,
our fall battered by carriers — clothing, books,
things from the past to help us into snow.

Undulant squirrels in the pushy grass,
like runabouts across the bay's bright
corner of shrinking sunshine, gather scraps
of paper, shoulder sparrows from their seed
and make their beds. I've never before
seen squirrels, except a red flick on an oak
on Fiesole, as leaves fell down like prayers.
I walked down later to Florence, your death —
thought of your death — a blizzard out of light,
battered my heart from mooring, scuppering
across a wide sky flaming with the glare
and clash of calvaries among the chestnuts.
Should a sparrow fall . . . The lock holds, the lock won't break
although I should break my timbers against the trunk.

10

And so each season has its stubborn death —
it's death makes summer fall, and winter creep
across Lake Erie, gripping Bethlehem's
steel playground cradle rack in an ice embrace.
Death ripens in the elms, the testament
scrawled out in gold. You fell, sideways,
on the sidewalk, a chopped elm, and bulk
immense and cruelly tiny under the sky.
Guide, stripped stick of punishment, lover
with a father's love — I'll sing you home
across inescapable distances and fear
to a bay's corner, where the rising sun
gilded the heart of darkness and you turned
and raced me into the water with a cheer.

Buffalo N.Y. October-December 1970

For my wife Fred

Magnificently naked
like a palm a coral beach
heaven at low tide
she lay on my bed and I said
to her 'Hello Fred'
to my wife and she
said 'Hi' although
she had never in her life spoken it before
so I said 'Hello' again
just to make sure and she
said 'Hi' and I looked
quizzically at her
and she said
'I'm magnificently naked
like a palm etc and
I'm not your wife.' I said
then 'Hi then' she said 'Higher'
together
we were heaven at high tide
we were magnificently like a palm
stirring the storm
we were a coral beach
I saw her
on my bed
she lay
I said to her
to my wife
'Hello' and she said
'Hello I've
come at last' looking
as though she had never in her life
spoken to me before.

Written late

Tired as an old truck
I know that I won't sleep tonight —
my family will come
to threaten and invite me on
along a rambling coast
— even the spindrift gulls are lost —
I've never seen but seems to lead
into my grandmother's bedroom.
It's not far now! You'll see it soon! —
they call, skirting a climbing hill.
I turn back, indecisive, while
the evening thickens, broods, and I
slip sideways to embrace the sea.

Tired as an abandoned dog,
as a burnt tree, charred log
on the slope of oblivion, waiting
nothing but a kind kick to go rolling
rolling into the lush fernery and deep-
fronded, murmuring hiding place of sleep,
I know that a man I've never seen
will camp by me, produce a book
and read long passages I want to look
at, stare thirstily on, memorize.
And when I have found my eyes,
stretched out my voice to him, he'll turn
back to his fire, and the book will burn.

Have you ever seen a bird fall?
— grandmother asks — Although all
birds out of their crystalline freeways must
one day plummet into dust,
have you ever seen a bird fall, as a man
tormented by insomnia will drown
at 4 a.m. on West

42nd Street in fathoms of air,
car-roof hammered to his pattern of despair?
My father has cages of birds within his palace
and hammered metal men who practise
the making of love with infinite degrees
of expertise and love and bitterness.

Their ballet clatters in the attic
a swift, insect arithmetic.
Somewhere between the Bering Straits
and southern Australia, from heights
unimaginable into the bland
tropical water's smiling hand,
migrating muttonbirds must fall,
their trackless homeless weariness
suddenly finding safe release.
Tired as a hunter, I would slip
into the close covert of sleep,
but I'll be called out over the depths
of living waves to catch their deaths.

Early winter

Everywhere in the thick valleys turning to sleep
snow blossoms on the ashes and the eyes
of hoar dentists laugh at children as they eat.
A ghost-plum in a thin hotel, left bitten,
the moon is a jackal whose orotund
obituaries of our loves sicken into tears.
Where are the ants? Why do the flies
fall like snow to lie in such a rich
harvest of loss at the slim ankles of the ash?
See where the whispering cars gather dusk
between sharp fingers of light, what do they
dream of when the wind rises at two?

A gull's shadow swoops, blotting into hot night
half a world — headlands ocean icecream-wrappings
with their scribble of eternity and childhood are not
redeemed by the Indian necklace of streetlamps
the tiara of elms processional among stars. No!
Who put the sea to bed? Who ate the coast?
Memory is a flurry of snow
where it has never snowed, it is the failure
of the present, it is a crow intoning in the skull
that we are not where we are, are not
a geography of salmon veins and shoals
but the shadow of a turning universe.

Somewhere a train pulls out from, into
a woman's smile. Handkerchiefs
blossom like cloud and become wings
the great sun in its forehead waxes and beams
all the ants in the sleepers rise up and sing
while the ashes bow gracefully low, naked as queens
in their new leaf.

Soon it will be snowing.

Twelve notions of Christmas

1

Sleet
scuffers the window
like the dry tenacious tinsel of an oak
in December
in a forgotten wind

2

Outside all ways all directions have been
scrubbed by the double dissolution of
night and snow
blackness and white
possess the land
clearly
it is an old conspiracy

3

This morning a squirrel's track across snow
sidling and darting
heavy step of a dog
paw paw paw paw paw after paw after paw
short cut of the newsboy over the lawn
were as much a part of morning as say
in late spring the bustle of leaves
rustling of bees
message of a thrush

4

My back
strained and aching like a curse
not through bearing any cross

but from shovelling snow
nails me upright in a chair
I hammer out words
on the bland blinding keyboard of winter
shadowy prints
stray in the direction of the sun

5

Nothing grows
in the Children's Hospital carpark
the cars of the doctors
huddle closer into earth
dreaming
in their white coats cocoons
of wings of flowers of breaking into tree

6

Before the snow melts
the Churches of America will again
be crucifying Christ
they should be expert
rehearsing on
small nation after small nation
which
dying
refuse to stay dead

7

After the President's message
and the Queen's message
and the Pope's message
after the hosanna in the highest and

after the eloi eloi lama sabachthani even
there will be the snow
like a blank page

8

A spot of blood on snow dawns on the world like grace

9

It is the colour of suffering it proclaims
life was here
between the last flurry and the next

10

Sleet has silenced to snow
always
this rinsing and cleaning
how white immaculate and still
the long dreams of the grass

11

There are no carols in stores like
the silence of snow
there is no silence
like that of a man contemplating snow

12

An ambulance wails in the dark
Children's Hospital or General Hospital
birth or death
birth and death
moving over the face of the snow
like light
like something spoken to a beloved

Unfinished sketch

Nothing is more frightening than a fresh canvas —
you once said — without feature blemish
waiting for you to
express the
beginning of a beginning

Nothing is more frightening —
I used to think — than a canvas
that had begun to grow
a design traced on it but not fleshed
a face a body a life
and been abandoned
turned from the light

Nothing is more frightening —
I'm beginning to think —
than to go back to take up
no not take up but to feel the weight of
the waiting of an abandoned sketch
to feel the lines grow firmer stronger more
binding
to feel the freedom of the line

to take up where you left off

World's End, Massachusetts

There, at the World's End, all ice and flame,
conclusions came so quick that life
leapt with pain, like a struck snake
through my smile. And would not die down.
On the frozen sea a labrador
skidded to retrieve a stick as my whole
life lost its footing — Here catch it! Quick —
out of control, trying not to change
direction, but my eyes were to you.
Not like that tree, tenacious to the rock
— Corny, you called its twisting — but a gull
slipping through emerald freeways, effortless,
flashing over ice, pure love, pure light,
that's how I wanted, how I want to be.
You whispered I love you, and I said the same.
Our kiss was flame across the ice, life
lashed and lashed till I had never known
such peace as then, your eyes closed, close to my cheek,
your hair miraculous in fire.
Such knowledge, and we departed, parted. It was
the World's End, like Eden, death in the heart.

New England pilgrimage

1

At Concord the temperature below zero
recalling Emerson that optimist for
Compensation
what did he know of loss
or the ultimate loss madness?
We live day to day
snow blowing from a branch
only leaves below ice
plan a revenge on winter
snow blowing through a hedge
light failing
it will get colder

2

Outside the car it is pure summer
at Marblehead the Atlantic the crisp
ocean spicker than a fleet of sails
in the January sun
ice cakes the shore pebbles of ice
green flagstones and the wind
honed where a mort of ships
lies drowned
Not swimming weather

3

The only witches in Salem
are in Florida because
it's winter not the tourist season
but they've left a spell
Nothing in this town will satisfy you
destitute
I can't even buy a sandwich

but that
isn't the hunger that traps me
gnawing
the heart from my travel

4

In the Berkshires breakfast was sold us by Dad
his hair was yellow from generations of hamburgers
he talked out of the twenties when perhaps he'd been
a young man selling hamburgers in the Berkshires
'This is the main highway here' I don't think
he'd even heard of the Massachusetts Turnpike

5

I gave you a film of ice ironically
'This is my love for you guard it carefully'
on the blinding shore World's End
it broke and you laughed you kissed me
the Prudential Building was a mere shade
you nibbled at the ice nothing
in my heart has been whole since
that winter melted all my resolve
my wife cries every time I kiss her

6

Coming back into New York
all the route-signs are wrong
everything points where I
don't want to go
the sun shines
mimicking when I held your hand and said
we mustn't bust our marriages for each other
Oh I'm so bright

I could get a job
cooking up hamburgers in the Berkshires

7

Last Sunday Niagara Falls
all that honeymooners' dream
plunging and boiling below an arid plateau
of ice
too many things I've left behind
only one really
about Concord
something in me froze
everything else plunges and demands

Seven years later

1

Every window I remember was filled with you
when your train left Florence
locked in with tears you could
not even wave to your friends but passed me
secretly like a brave handkerchief
the helpless compassion of misery
I cried all the way to London
people in the compartment gave me something to eat
I knew how you felt

2

Seven years later I knew where I was going
I wrote you of it the first
look again I was a fire at sea
I'd lied to myself about the meltingpoint of ice

3

I'm farther back in Rome you
argue you're not erotic in the morning I
argue you're not erotic at all
we'd found
fondo and it was
as we'd expected
full of Germans with maps
they were trying to get out
Romulus
couldn't arbitrate we can't
jump over this wall

4

The Forum was hollow with tunnels and every
tunnel we had to kiss in
also
last week by the silent frozen sea we
oh it was no joke my
iceflow melted was shot from under me
big bear went down like a stone I want to
hunt out a bear and climb inside instead
this one's drowning he
doesn't even speak with your tongue
how does he call help
how does he call help

5

I'm no hunter I remember
the first rabbit I ever shot it turned
slowly on its shoulder and looked
at me your eyes
I had to shoot it in the head it
watched me not the rifle
which of us died

6

When thaw comes the little huts
left by the ice-fishers if they're not wary
are trapped by the breakup are
swept off maybe
I'll even see one hurling over Niagara
nobody sitting on the can but at least
a dozen different tackles a bottle
of whisky a flashlight and a shovel descend
like some nut in a barrel

over the whirlpool under the ice
is that what's happening
too patient too timid maybe
there's a tide somewhere in the affairs of man
it seems to be sucking down or flooding oh
all I need is your hand
no
facile solutions like
'how to be an accessory after a rescue'

7

I love you

Please don't enter without knocking

1

Why do you keep haunting me
surely in this trinity
one of us deserves rest?

You Roberta I passed a whole day
not thinking of you
your grey eyes didn't peel me like a scalpel
through the smoke and drinks
and effortless politenesses to strangers
probe at the taut snake in my heart
his glittering gold mail
'the pure being' somebody called it
my tensed spring at the heart of winter
(you were afraid
your eyes were entranced and afraid yes I saw that too

nor you John
my father I didn't think of you
a few months dead of your heart
thousands of miles dead I shall return
to nothing but a grave and that
not even where I live

I thought instead of my wife
a whole day my thoughts walked with her through the snow
what blossoms winter hung there in the trees
what flowers crackled from ice

2

I stood with you on your pier
your son playing on the ice below
we discussed the hideous movie that a malign
director with a flair for scenery had trapped us in

including later the invitation for Easter
from your mother
(masterly irony there
enough was being strung out
that would not die
that would not stay buried under snow

3

It would surely have been mother asked me to find knive
in the pantry where the surplus cutlery
lay like an infant's dream of luxury

No it was you John last night all night
searching for knives I was the knives' victim
nothing to be found I was so impotent

The last I saw you I didn't kiss goodbye
leaving you to die I shook hands manfully
none of my love for you firmed that public clutch

(Three months before I'd seen your life as a faint
blunder across a screen while your heart crept
amplified and tremulous across unthinkable gaps

4

Blazing snow
yesterday
I was my wife's
myself
Lake Erie frozen across
Niagara Falls still hurled
on bare twig blanched wood
a whole summer of light

If it can do that we asked
why can't the whole mist freeze
like a loaf a souffle in air
high to the bright sky?

Under the ice
nothing tranquil nor clear
although the ice bridged even

5

Almost asleep a hand tugs at
the horizon draws me through it into
a room where we are holding hands
your husband and my wife are
with dark frightened bones not
seeing where we are
and my father merely falling in the street
dead before he hits the ground
killed at the heart he just drops limp

6

Daring your neighbours we stand hand to hand
your son plays on the ice
I have no children
my wife and I walk through a snow like fire

7

I am too tired to argue with you both
leave me alone I pray please let me go
with you father I went down
with you Roberta I grew up
again against you I grew strong

(not strong enough or too strong which was it?)
together Jill and I walk through mist
and feel the shudder below the ice
and watch ice angels on the twigs

no not too tired now maybe too sure

I'll meet you in my home now not yours
when you come I intend to say Wait till I open
I love you both
but from now on you'll be my guests mine and my wife's
a whole day I've kept you loose from our life
I intend to keep you out there in the snow
till it suits us to let you in
please don't enter without knocking again
and please
don't go away

Sunday morning

Since yesterday it's been snowing
tyretracks are white trails
perilous
weather to be driving
(wolves' howl sirens' yelp a trapped car)

Walking downtown with my ghosts
suddenly there is sun no not
blue sky but the
swirling atmosphere burns burgeons is alive
acres fathoms of it bustling and ablaze
(underwater I dive upward into
the sky the sun's foil everything expands
explodes into

No
I can't touch your face
even approach your dear body
friends father yes they die
but I am happy that I love you
my wife my father and my lover
happy that I love you all
the sun
fills air with the petals of almonds
the blizzard blossoms toward spring
out from our fire and snow
it weeps like a miracle

February
and so many things are alive

The ice fishermen, Lake Erie

Beside the steel plant
washed by sulphurous smoke
no sea wings
no clatter of beaks nor the sharp
antagonism of cries
no soughing of pines not even
the scribble and rage of ti-tree across cliffs
no scramble of dunes
no suck and hiss on the sand
no clink of shells
no shells
no sand

only the orange smoke spreading from stacks
only the shadows hurled across ice
the black forest of the steel plant
the cindered roads the wiry spike-riddled fence
the buffered ends
of the steel company railroad
the channel for freighters
the long-legged
meandering stride of the skyway humped over docks
slumped into swamps

the evening orange as the late light
blazes through smoke and steam from the steel plant
wings of smoke swoop darkly and glide off
somewhere out on the lake
the ghost of a breeze invokes the ghost of a flurry

as though they were skaters
as though they were fixed in nightmare on the ice
as though the music had stopped and each
bent in a miserly gesture towards hell
as though in a picnic on the ice

they had taken root
like the steel plant
on the ice on the dead lake they are

of all things they are fishing
fishing for fish
or the mercury trapped in the flesh
in the glands of the few poor
whatever lampreys could live there in the stench
and run-off from the steel plant
would they eat what they catch?

do they catch fish at all?

it being Sunday maybe this is really
an aspiration to hope
hope that beneath the ice something's thrashing and hungry
butting toward the sky just as they crouch
hunched over dark
hope that in the shadow of the steel plant
the hunger trapping them could be dragged up
into that air out of that lake

hope that they'll meet themselves there face to face
one drowning in air
feeding those huddled bodies that confront
that dying in air

Sunburnt in May

Two winters melt under my skin
yes the lake's broken but like a drink in a bar
it's mostly ice
wind bitches the roofs

but I can pass the dead woman in the field
I can laugh at the crow flapping his eye at the north
I can sing bass to the frozen hedge's treble
for it's flying green flags now and her dress ripples

Spring was oddly mislayed
summer has caught me unaware
kissed by the dead I'm suddenly bright as flame
I'll challenge the crow to vocals anyday

his comment on my rise falls like a flailed snake
a woman in the hedges whispers night's near
ice still chokes the falls
but sun has mounted my thigh and the night comes clear

Memorial Day, U.S.A. 1971

As I move downstairs I hear singing
in the cellar they're burning a baby to charcoal
the mothers and the fathers singing of sacrifice

and as I move upstairs I hear the hatching of birds
the scrabble of baby squirrels among leaves
the cleaning of shotguns the oiling of rifles

and Ives's variations on My Country, 'Tis of Thee
everyone falls into fountains or flat on lawns
cops lean on their pistols because it's the land of the free

Annihilating all things made

Whenever the green shade lowered or the shade
of the magnolia beside the tennis court
the tall pines and in the street the dogs
like shetland ponies oh how afraid
of the clothesline watch your head out riding
my neck like a sock hung up there to dry
in the dessicating winter sun
so many miles from the nearest hidingplace I

(that was winter we'd driven through floods
axle deep for over fifty miles
rabbits swam to us they were so exhausted and sheep
were a wet huddle of footrot I was a wonderful duck
water tickling my foot one boot in a burrow)

but whenever the green shade in the street went down
whenever the black pines beside the court
or the swimming pool (many years later)
or snow doesn't come when oak leaves are black
not gold in winter or when it's hot
and the heart's comments are thunder nothing but bruise

Do go riding with your cousins you like horses
Do go out and play with the dogs you like dogs
Do go out in the water shooting rabbits you like rabbits
It's time for you to play tennis now you want to play tennis

over the swimmingpool on a hot night
pines loose their bombs I could be lying there
on a hot day I've seen a magnolia split
boughs collapse flowers explode in the heat
chips splinters factory girls who were sitting
panicked all terror running yelping one fainted
none of them killed none raped
while the green shade went down on the one that fainted

in the middle of summer she was lying drifting
in a cool pool she was quite surrounded by rabbits
holes drilled tidily through their faces shivering sheep

and I'm asked to find my tennis racquet
the hallway's crowded with pines
nothing in its right mind swims in my direction
snow suffocates the grandfather clock
the oaks are all in the refrigerator and they're not
my cousins gallop down the stairs twirling a clothesline

oh it's wonderfully cool here in the shade
cool as a hand on my fever over my eyes my mouth
while the sun's just a few miles off buying everybody drink

In praise of weeping outdoors

You can weep into the
unvarnished air it will
usher you into estuaries of elms
oaks' puzzle of dark

you will flow out like milk of a Madonna
in a Flemish village
ugly and sanctified
by a cow's attention

you will be a strayed storm with a centre
as big as your heart
the whole world may blur to your season
oaks elms chestnuts will attend

they will reach for your tears
something about them will never say
you're a mere foolish creature

not while your tears nest in them
green leaf upon green leaf
you can weep into the air and the air

is what we don't see, it is
the world's apology for not being us

it is unseen, and secret, like a friend

That silence

Finally

silence

not even the dumb butting of snow on
dark air
nor the mute
nakedness of twigs waiting for spring
nor the rich earthy music of stone
as in mothering mud
it nuzzles farther from the sun
not even the chatter of stars
nor the slow
ambiguous
basses of clouds mountains ocean
not even
the dazzling song of ice in shrill air
nor a slant
sun's
innuendo

but

behind it all
crouched somewhere in your eyes
darker than love than concentration
that sobbing terrible hymn that you will never hear
curled like an infant
in the black
back of your eyes

somewhere within you
you
oh
so utterly silent